HONORING THE CALL
WORKBOOK

Deborah Dancy & Monica Drish

REJOICE
Essential Publishing

Deborah Dancy & Monica Drish/Rejoice Essential Publishing
PO BOX 512
Effingham, SC 29541
www.republishing.org

Honoring the Call Workbook/Deborah Dancy & Monica Drish

ISBN-13: 978-1-956775-85-3

TABLE OF CONTENTS

CHAPTER 1

TO HONOR

What does the Word of God say according to John 5:23?

_____

_____

_____

_____

_____

_____

_____

_____

_____

_____

_____

Honor is all about who and why? List and expound on two scriptures that speak to your statement. _____

_____

_____

_____

_____

_____

_____

_____

_____

_____

_____

_____

_____

_____

_____

_____

_____

_____

_____

Read and write out Deuteronomy 6:13 and provide your understanding of this verse..

_____

_____

_____

_____

_____

_____

_____

_____

_____

_____

_____

_____

_____

_____

_____

_____

_____

Discuss three scriptures that speaks to how we are to worship God.

_____

_____

_____

_____

_____

_____

_____

_____

_____

_____

_____

_____

_____

_____

_____

_____

_____

_____

_____

_____

_____

_____

_____

List and discuss three scriptures that speaks to the benefits of worshipping God. _____

_____

_____

_____

_____

_____

_____

_____

_____

_____

_____

_____

_____

_____

_____

_____

_____

_____

List things or people that we worship before God and why.

List at least three ways to honor God, please use scriptural references. _____

_____

_____

_____

_____

_____

_____

_____

_____

_____

_____

_____

_____

_____

_____

_____

_____

_____

_____

In Chapter 1, the author stated "The biggest tragedy that one could express, is to hear

a call from _____

_____

_____ and not God."

What does honor mean to you?

_____

_____

_____

_____

_____

_____

_____

_____

_____

_____

After reading Deuteronomy 6:13, what can you change?

_____

_____

_____

_____

_____

_____

_____

_____

_____

_____

_____

_____

_____

What are the definitions for committed and submitted?

_____

_____

_____

_____

_____

_____

_____

_____

List and expound on two scriptures that relates to how we are to commit and submit

to God.

_____

_____

_____

_____

_____

_____

_____

_____

_____

_____

_____

_____

_____

_____

_____

_____

_____

_____

Do you have time set aside to commune with God? What do you do during this time?

_____

_____

_____

_____

_____

_____

_____

_____

_____

_____

_____

_____

_____

_____

Write down a time that you did not honor the voice of God, what would you do differently?

_____

_____

_____

_____

_____

_____

Have you ever disrespected or dishonored a leader, parent, brother, or sister in Christ?

How did you make it right?

_____

_____

_____

_____

_____

_____

_____

_____

_____

_____

_____

_____

_____

_____

_____

_____

What does submission and humility mean? Provide and write out a scriptural reference

for each.

_____

_____

_____

_____

_____

_____

_____

_____

_____

_____

_____

_____

_____

_____

_____

_____

_____

_____

_____

_____

_____

_____

_____

_____

_____

Fill in the blank.

_____ yourself, then, under God's

(Peter 5:6-7, James 4:6, James 4:10, Peter 5:2, Chronicles 7:14, Prov 11:2, Prov 15:33,

Prov 18:12, Prov 22:4, Philip 2:3-4).

Elaborate on Philippians 2:3 _____

_____

_____

_____

_____

_____

_____

_____

_____

_____

_____

Please summarize three key points from Chapter 1.

_____

_____

_____

_____

_____

_____

_____

CHAPTER 2

THE SUMMON

What is a Summon? _____

_____

_____

_____

_____

_____

How does God summons us? _____

_____

_____

_____

_____

_____

_____

_____

_____

_____

_____

_____

_____

Describe ways in which we take the summon of God lightly. _____

_____

_____

_____

_____

_____

_____

_____

_____

_____

_____

_____

_____

_____

How is a call like a summon? _____

_____

_____

_____

_____

_____

_____

_____

_____

_____

_____

_____

Share ways in which God calls you? Provide two scriptural references.

_____

_____

_____

_____

_____

_____

_____

_____

_____

_____

_____

_____

_____

_____

_____

_____

Describe examples of these individuals, their call, and their response. (Moses, Samuel, and Jonah) _____

_____

_____

_____

_____

_____

_____

_____

_____

_____

_____

_____

_____

_____

_____

_____

_____

_____

_____

Write the definition of magnitude and relate it to God's call/summon.

_____

_____

_____

_____

_____

_____

_____

_____

_____

_____

_____

_____

_____

What voice have you put before the Voice of God?

_____

_____

_____

_____

_____

_____

_____

_____

_____

_____

_____

_____

_____

_____

_____

What is the definition of submission? How do we submit to God? Provide scripture references.

_____

_____

_____

_____

_____

_____

_____

_____

_____

_____

_____

_____

_____

_____

_____

_____

_____

_____

Write the definition of remission?

_____

_____

_____

_____

_____

_____

List excuses we use/used for not submitting. Discuss one person in the Bible, who did

not want to submit to the voice of God.

_____

_____

_____

_____

_____

_____

_____

_____

_____

_____

_____

_____

In your own words expound on Deuteronomy Chapter 13.

_____

_____

_____

_____

_____

_____

_____

_____

_____

_____

_____

_____

_____

_____

_____

_____

_____

_____

_____

_____

Describe the wrestling against the summon, according to 2 Corinthians 10:3-5.

_____

_____

_____

_____

_____

_____

_____

_____

_____

_____

_____

_____

_____

_____

_____

_____

_____

_____

_____

_____

What does the Bible say in Galatians 3:28 and 2 Timothy 1:9? Does God show partiality as to whom He calls/summons?

_____

_____

_____

_____

_____

_____

_____

_____

_____

_____

_____

_____

_____

_____

_____

Please summarize three key points from Chapter 2.

_____

_____

_____

_____

CHAPTER 3

THE CALL

Why is the call necessary?

_____

_____

_____

_____

_____

_____

_____

_____

What is the definition of necessary?

_____

_____

_____

_____

_____

_____

What is the difference between failed and setback?

_____

_____

_____

_____

_____

_____

_____

Explain 2 Timothy 1:9-10 as it relates to God calling us.

_____

_____

_____

_____

_____

_____

_____

_____

_____

_____

_____

God calls us before the _____

_____ of the _____

_____.

What are reasons we ignore the call?

_____

_____

_____

_____

_____

_____

_____

_____

_____

_____

_____

Have you ever heard that the call was not necessary? Why?

_____

_____

_____

_____

_____

_____

_____

_____

What visions did God give Isaiah in Isaiah Chapter 6 and Joseph in Genesis 37?

_____

_____

_____

_____

_____

_____

_____

_____

_____

_____

_____

_____

_____

_____

Who did the author mentioned went forth without a call from God? Please site the scripture What happened to them? Why did it happen to them?

_____

_____

_____

_____

_____

_____

_____

_____

_____

_____

_____

_____

_____

_____

_____

_____

_____

_____

Why did Jesus cry out in John Chapter 15?

_____

_____

_____

_____

_____

_____

_____

_____

_____

_____

_____

_____

_____

_____

Why did He cry this out?

- -

- -

- -

- -

- -

Has He ever cried out to you? How did you respond to His cry?

_____

_____

_____

_____

_____

_____

_____

_____

_____

_____

What does it mean to be fruitful?

_____

_____

_____

_____

_____

_____

_____

List three scriptures and discuss the meaning of bearing fruit.

_____

_____

_____

_____

_____

_____

_____

_____

_____

_____

_____

_____

_____

_____

_____

What does it mean to bear fruit?

_____

_____

_____

_____

_____

_____

_____

_____

_____

Discuss a time when you felt like you were being tested or tried. What did you learn?

_____

_____

_____

_____

_____

_____

_____

_____

_____

_____

What fruit do you feel that people were able to see while you were being tested or tried?

_____

_____

_____

_____

_____

_____

_____

List the scripture reference and the nine fruits of the Spirit.

_____

_____

_____

_____

_____

_____

_____

_____

_____

_____

_____

Have you ever had to deal with people spreading rumors about you? How did you deal with them?

_____

_____

_____

_____

_____

_____

_____

_____

_____

_____

What does it mean to multiply and replenish the earth? How can you do this?

_____

_____

_____

_____

_____

_____

_____

_____

_____

_____

Please summarize three key points from Chapter 3

_____

_____

_____

_____

_____

_____

_____

_____

_____

_____

_____

CHAPTER 4

THE CHOSEN

What does it mean to resolve something in your heart? Have you ever had to resolve an issue in your heart? Explain the step you took to resolve.

_____

_____

_____

_____

_____

_____

_____

_____

_____

_____

_____

_____

What condition do you think that you as "The Chosen One" will have to comply to? Please list scriptures to support your statement.

_____

_____

_____

_____

_____

_____

_____

_____

_____

_____

_____

_____

_____

_____

_____

_____

_____

_____

How will you comply to this condition?

_____

_____

_____

_____

_____

_____

Define foreknowledge.

_____

_____

_____

_____

_____

_____

_____

_____

_____

_____

What does God having a foreknowledge mean? Please provide two scriptural references.

_____

_____

_____

_____

_____

_____

_____

_____

_____

_____

_____

_____

_____

_____

_____

_____

_____

_____

Matthew 22:14 reads "For many are called but few are chosen." What is the difference between called and chosen?

_____

_____

_____

_____

_____

_____

_____

_____

_____

_____

_____

_____

_____

_____

_____

_____

Which scriptures tell us to make our calling (election) sure? How do you make your election sure?

_____

_____

_____

_____

_____

_____

_____

_____

_____

_____

_____

_____

_____

_____

_____

_____

_____

How do you continue to honor your call in the face of rejection or overcoming past mistakes? Please list scriptures to support your statement.

_____

_____

_____

_____

_____

_____

_____

_____

_____

_____

_____

_____

_____

_____

_____

_____

_____

_____

List three individuals from the Bible who were rejected, however they honored their call. Please provide scriptural references, discuss how were they rejected , and how did they overcome the rejection.

_____

_____

Please summarize three key points from Chapter 4.

_____

_____

_____

_____

_____

_____

_____

_____

_____

_____

_____

_____

_____

_____

_____

_____

_____

_____

_____

_____

_____

_____

_____

_____

_____

_____

_____

_____

_____

_____

_____

_____

_____

_____

_____

CHAPTER 5

THE TESTING

Please explain Deuteronomy Chapter 13 as it relates to honoring the call. Does God evaluate your motives as it relates to honor? Explain.

_____

_____

_____

_____

_____

_____

_____

_____

_____

_____

_____

_____

_____

_____

_____

_____

_____

_____

_____

_____

_____

Please list and discuss anything that has tried to keep you from following what God commanded you to do.

_____

_____

_____

_____

_____

_____

_____

_____

_____

_____

_____

_____

_____

_____

_____

List and discuss with scriptural references, commands of God.

_____

_____

_____

_____

_____

_____

_____

_____

_____

_____

_____

_____

_____

_____

_____

_____

_____

_____

What does it mean in 2 Timothy 4:5, to make full proof of your ministry?

_____

_____

_____

_____

_____

_____

_____

_____

_____

_____

_____

_____

_____

_____

_____

After reading this book, what will you do to help draw others into a relationship with God?

_____

_____

_____

_____

_____

_____

_____

_____

_____

_____

_____

What are you doing each day to stay connected to the God as your source.

_____

_____

_____

_____

_____

_____

_____

_____

_____

_____

_____

_____

Look up Ephesians 2:9 and write it out and discuss your understanding of it.

_____

_____

_____

_____

_____

_____

_____

_____

_____

_____

_____

_____

_____

_____

_____

What does it mean to be ceremonially clean? Provide scriptural reference. How does it

apply to honoring your call?

_____

_____

_____

_____

_____

_____

_____

_____

_____

_____

_____

_____

_____

_____

_____

Read and write out John Chapter 5:7 and provide your understanding of it.

_____

_____

_____

_____

_____

_____

_____

_____

_____

_____

_____

_____

_____

_____

_____

_____

Please summarize three key points from Chapter 5.

_____

_____

_____

_____

_____

_____

_____

_____

_____

CHAPTER 6

THE URGENCY

How do we make full proof of our ministries? Provide scriptural references.

_____

_____

_____

_____

_____

_____

_____

_____

_____

_____

_____

_____

_____

_____

What things do you need to do to equip yourself to honor what God has called you to do?

_____

_____

_____

_____

_____

_____

_____

_____

_____

_____

_____

_____

What is humility? What is humble? Compare and contrast humility and humble. Provide two scriptures on being humble.

_____

_____

_____

_____

_____

_____

_____

_____

_____

_____

_____

_____

_____

_____

_____

_____

_____

_____

_____

_____

Have you ever felt like God could not use you? Why?

_____

_____

_____

_____

_____

_____

_____

_____

_____

_____

_____

Are there things that you feel unrested about? Please explain why.

_____

_____

_____

_____

_____

_____

_____

_____

_____

_____

_____

_____

What do you imagine yourself doing for the Lord?

_____

_____

_____

_____

_____

_____

_____

_____

_____

_____

_____

_____

_____

_____

_____

_____

Write out Psalm 139:16, Ephesians 5:16, and Titus 3:8. Please provide your understanding of each.

_____

_____

_____

_____

_____

_____

_____

_____

_____

_____

_____

_____

_____

_____

_____

_____

_____

_____

_____

_____

The author stated in Chapter 6, that the urgency, brings you to the realization that God

_____

_____

_____. God blew the_____

_____

_____! This urgency causes _____

_____

_____.

Please summarize three key points from Chapter 6.

_____

_____

_____

_____

_____

_____

_____

CHAPTER 7

THE PREDESTINED

What is the definition of preordained?

_____

_____

_____

_____

_____

_____

Read and write out Ephesians 1:3. How do you apply it to honoring the call?

_____

_____

_____

_____

_____

_____

_____

_____

_____

_____

_____

_____

Read Exodus 3:1-4, 3:11-12, and write it out and discuss its implications on honoring what God called you to do.

_____

_____

_____

_____

_____

_____

_____

_____

_____

_____

_____

_____

_____

_____

_____

_____

_____

_____

_____

Have there ever been voices that interfered with your obedience to God? How did you respond?

_____

_____

_____

_____

_____

_____

_____

_____

_____

_____

_____

_____

_____

_____

_____

How do you pull down from the heavenly realm? Please provide scriptural references.

_____

_____

_____

_____

_____

_____

_____

_____

_____

_____

_____

_____

_____

_____

_____

Explain what the author said about predestined and adoption on page 29 of Honoring the Call.

_____

_____

_____

_____

_____

_____

_____

_____

_____

_____

_____

_____

Discus where you are in Honoring what God called you to do. Are you at a place of

maturity? Explain why or why not?

_____

_____

_____

_____

_____

_____

_____

_____

_____

_____

_____

_____

_____

_____

_____

Read and write out Matthew 5:6. Please provide your understanding of this scripture.

_____

_____

_____

_____

_____

_____

_____

_____

_____

_____

_____

_____

Read and write out John 4:24. Please provide your understanding of this scripture.

_____

_____

_____

_____

_____

_____

_____

_____

_____

_____

_____

_____

_____

_____

_____

Read and write out Jeremiah 31:3. Please provide your understanding of this scripture.

_____

_____

_____

_____

_____

_____

_____

_____

_____

_____

_____

_____

_____

_____

Read and write out 1 Peter 2:2 (NLT). Please provide your understanding of this scripture.

_____

_____

_____

_____

_____

_____

_____

_____

_____

_____

Read and write Romans 8:9-11. Please provide your understanding of these verses.

_____

_____

_____

_____

_____

_____

_____

_____

_____

_____

_____

_____

_____

_____

_____

_____

_____

_____

_____

_____

_____

_____

_____

_____

_____

What is God's anointing? Provide scriptures to support your answer.

_____

_____

_____

_____

_____

_____

_____

_____

_____

_____

_____

_____

What have you done to put yourself in a place to grow spiritually?

_____

_____

_____

_____

_____

_____

_____

_____

_____

_____

_____

_____

_____

_____

_____

What is dunamis power? Provide scriptures. How was it used and what was the results.

_____

_____

_____

_____

_____

_____

_____

_____

_____

_____

_____

_____

_____

_____

_____

Please summarize three key points from Chapter 7.

_____

_____

_____

_____

_____

_____

_____

_____

_____

_____

_____

_____

_____

CHAPTER 8

THE PAST

What does it mean to have a past?

_____

_____

_____

_____

_____

_____

_____

Are there things in the past that you have not let go of? If so, why?

_____

_____

_____

_____

_____

_____

_____

_____

_____

_____

_____

Read and write out Philippians 3:12-14. Please provide your understanding of these verses.

_____

_____

_____

_____

_____

_____

_____

_____

_____

_____

_____

_____

_____

_____

_____

_____

_____

Read and write out Corinthians 4:7. Please provide your understanding of this verse.

_____

_____

_____

_____

_____

_____

_____

_____

_____

_____

_____

_____

Read and write out Jeremiah 1:4. Please provide your understanding of this verse.

_____

_____

_____

_____

_____

_____

_____

_____

_____

_____

_____

_____

_____

_____

_____

Read and write out Luke 22:42. Please provide your understanding of this verse.

_____

_____

_____

_____

_____

_____

_____

_____

_____

_____

_____

_____

_____

_____

_____

Read and write out Ezekiel 36:36, Jeremiah 31:33, and Hebrew 8:10. Please provide your understanding of these scriptures.

_____

_____

_____

_____

_____

_____

_____

_____

_____

_____

_____

_____

_____

_____

_____

_____

_____

Please summarize three key points from Chapter 8.

_____

_____

_____

_____

_____

_____

_____

_____

_____

_____

_____

_____

_____

_____

_____

_____

_____

_____

_____

_____

_____

_____

_____

_____

_____

_____

_____

_____

_____

_____

Take away the stony heart and give us a heart of flesh!

APOSTLE DR. DEBORAH DANCY

Founder of Deborah Dancy Ministries, Loosed to Hear Inc., and Jehovah Shalom International Kingdom Ministries, located in Bessemer AL and Sierra Leone West Africa

Dr. Deborah Dancy, daughter of Ms. Sadie Dancy, attended Birmingham City Schools. Graduating in the top ten percent of her high school graduating class, she received the *Who's Who American High School Students Award* for academic excellence. After graduating High School, Dr. Dancy attended Lawson State, Birmingham Southern and the University of Alabama at Birmingham, earning an undergraduate degree in Early Childhood Education and Social Psychology, with a minor in Social Work. Graduating with honors, she also earned a master's degree in biblical counseling and Doctoral Degree in December 2010.

Dr. Dancy was the recipient of the National Dean's List, UAB Sociology Honor's Program. Dr. Dancy was recommended by the UAB Sociology Department and accepted to be inducted into Alpha Kappa Delta Sociological Honor's Society, whereas only 10% of Sociology students are asked to join.

Dr. Dancy retired from the Department of Veterans Affairs in Birmingham, Alabama as the Director Clinic Administration, in March of 2021 with a total of thirty-three years of service to America's heroes.

Dr. Dancy is the Senior Founding Pastor of Jehovah Shalom International Kingdom Ministries, Bessemer, Alabama. In October of 2020, she planted her first church in Sierra Leone, West Africa.

Dr. Dancy is the founder of Sadie Dancy Academy in Sierra Leone, West Africa, providing primary education to students who cannot afford the education fees in their village., the school open its doors to students in September 2023. Dr. Dancy named the school in honor of her mother Sadie Dancy, who instilled the value of education in the lives of her children, resulting in all being college educated.

Dr. Dancy is the Chancellor and founder of Jehovah Shalom International Kingdom Ministries Training College, equipping the body of Christ for their God given assignment, through licensing and ordaining, after completing required courses and ministry projects.

Dr. Dancy is the Chancellor of Jehovah Shalom International Kingdom Ministries Theological Seminary, which is an accredited school, offering the following degrees: Associate, Bachelor's, Master's and Doctoral in theology. The Seminary will open in the Spring of 2024 and will be an online program.

Dr. Dancy was Ordained as an Apostle in Stockholm Sweden in October of 2011, by Apostle Alex Ngabo. The late Bishop Earnest Palmer licensed and ordained Dr. Dancy at Cornerstone Full Gospel Baptist Church., in Tuscaloosa, Alabama, as a minister in 2000, and as an elder in 2001.

While a member of Cornerstone, she taught Sunday school and served as Evangelism Instructor. A certified Prison Fellowship Instructor, Dr. Dancy facilitated weekly Bible Studies at the Tuscaloosa Youth Detention Center under the auspices of Prison Fellowship Ministries and Cornerstone Evangelism Ministry. She also facilitated these sessions at Ross Detention in Birmingham.

Dr. Dancy is a past Board Secretary for Big Brothers Big Sisters of the Greater Birmingham area, where she actively served for six years. She is past recipient of the Big Sister of the Year Award, and
mentored four little sisters through the Big Brothers/Big Sisters Program, with a total of twelve years of volunteer service.

Dr. Dancy presently serves on the Board of Directors for Alabama Regional Medical Services (ARMS), where she serves as the Chair of the Personnel Committee and member of the Quality Assurance Committee.

In April of 2004, Dr. Dancy was nominated by Birmingham's VA's leadership and selected by the nominating committee as Birmingham's VA Woman of The Year, during its annual program of spotlighting a deserving male and female for services rendered to the Department of Veterans Affairs and the community.

Dr. Dancy was nominated and selected out of 165 nominations for the 2004 Excellence in EFNEP (Expanded Food & Nutrition Education Program). On March 2, 2004, EFNEP celebrated its 35th Anniversary in Washington DC at the Dirksen Senate Office Building. During that time, the twenty-four winners were recognized. Dr. Dancy not only received the Excellence in EFNEP Award, which was awarded by the United States Department of Agriculture, but she was also presented a Special Congressional Award, a Proclamation from the House of Congress. Lastly, Dr. Dancy's name will be listed in the Congressional Book of Records. Congressman Artur Davis attended the award ceremony and presented Dr. Dancy with each of these awards. Congressman Davis made special mention in his proclamation, highlighting her community and civic involvement.

Upon Dr. Dancy's return from Washington DC, Dr. Dancy, EFNEP nominated and selected Dr. Dancy as the State's recipient of EFNEP award, presented at Auburn University in August of 2004. Congressman Artur Davis was the keynote speaker.

A community activist, Dr. Dancy is often requested to speak at various women day programs and conferences. She has been the keynote speaker on various occasions for the Alabama Cooperative Extension Center Programs. Of note, she was their Keynote Speaker at the National Conference in St. Louis Missouri.

On March 14, 2008, Deborah Glenn Ministries Inc., currently known as Deborah Dancy Ministries (DDM), was unveiled at The Birmingham Botanical Gardens with a record number in attendance. One of the entities of Deborah Dancy Ministries Inc. is Loosed To H-E-A-R (Healed & Delivered, Empowered, Anchored and Restored) Ministries Inc., a 501c (3) organization, which focuses on the Youthful Offender and the At Risk. The premise of this ministry is to empower the "at risk youth," back to a place of wholeness, with the Word of God being the foundation.

Dr. Dancy's 501c3in conjunction with DDM, ministry is presently working to build a school and an orphanage for children affected by the Civil War in Sierra Leone West Africa. She had the opportunity to visit Sierra Leone in October 2012, where she conducted empowerment conferences and leadership workshops and while there, Dr. Dancy had the opportunity to deliver empowerment messages via radio covering Africa and surrounding Europe, reaching an audience of over five million people.

Dr. Dancy and her team travelled to Sierra Leone, West Africa in May of 2023, where her organization has purchased property and have started building the much-needed orphanage.

Dr. Dancy published her first book in October 2020, "Honoring the Call", Dr. Dancy's book is presently being taught in churches and Bible -study groups across the United States, the workbook to "Honoring the Call", with co-author Monica Drish, will be published in the Winter of 2024.

Dr. Dancy has ordained over 50 Ministers, including placing more than half in the 5-Fold Ministry office; and currently has approximately seventeen students enrolled in JSIKM Training College, where she presides as Chancellor.

Dr. Deborah Dancy's motto is: "To run with endurance the race set before her, fixing her eyes on Jesus."

APOSTLE MONICA DRISH

Monica Drish is the mother of one daughter and the grandmother of one granddaughter, while also operating as the Founder and CEO of P.U.S.H. @ 4 am Prayer Ministry, founded upon the scripture, "as iron sharpens iron, so a friend sharpens a friend" Proverbs 27:17 (NLT). Through this ministry, she and a group of exceptional leaders make one of the most significant spiritual impacts through relentless prayer and intercession. By committing to staying on their post, without fail, at 4 am, P.U.S.H. Ministries stands in the gap until they witness the manifestation of divine intervention in the lives of those they serve, in addition to their loved ones, friends, community, government, church, nation, and the world.

The fourth of seven children, Monica was born to the Late Melvin Drish and JoAnn Drish, and at an early age, she began to develop her love for reading, shopping, skating, and music. After graduating from Glenville High School in Cleveland, Ohio, Monica graduated from Rice College, becoming a Master Manager Cosmetologist to train others in the art of Cosmetology as an instructor at Minor High School.

Despite her willingness to selflessly serve others, Monica heard the call of God and His desire for her to do more within His Kingdom. Honoring the call, she became a licensed and ordained Minister at More Than Conquerors Faith Church under the leadership of Apostle Steve Green in 2000, where she served as the leader of Special Hospitality and a member of the Pastoral care and intake team. Monica then obtained a certificate in Lay Counseling in 2010 from Stephen Ministries to supplement her Pastoral Care experience while under the leadership of Bishop Vann Moody, Senior Pastor of The Worship Center Christian Church. Following this and continually heeding God's voice, Monica began to take on various roles within the church, including:

- Prayer Leader across three church campuses and leading 156 Prayer Team members
- Leader of Small Groups Development
- Leader of Baptism
- Small Groups Coach
- Leader of the New Members' Training curriculum
- A member of the Launch Team that helped to plant a church campus in Anniston, Alabama

In addition to serving as Campus Pastor, who was responsible for opening and closing Sunday services, Monica aided in Pulpit Ministry, performed altar calls, and administered Communion. Feeling a push to delve deeper into the Heavenly assignment placed upon her life, Monica enrolled in and graduated from Highlands College in 2018, obtaining a Certificate in Ministry under the Leadership of Senior Pastor Chris Hodges. Subsequently, Monica continued her Kingdom mission by serving as a Small Group Leader for over 50 groups and saw God move in the lives of thousands of people. While functioning as a Small Groups coach, Monica gained the opportunity to serve as a member of the Events team, Prayer Team, and Intercessory Prayer Team for conferences.

During the pandemic, Monica became an online member of the Potter's House, Dallas, after realizing an inner desire for further wisdom and knowledge. Ultimately, it was under the leadership of Bishop T.D. Jakes, in addition to his unyielding and steadfast anointing, whose words reverberated within Monica's spirit and acted as a newfound stability in her life amidst the turbulence of the time. However, God would later place Hebrews 10:25 (NLT) in her heart, which says, "… and let us not neglect our meeting together, as some people do, but encourage one another, especially now that the day of his return is drawing near". Soon afterwards, Monica sought fellowship with Jehovah Shalom International Kingdom Ministries under the leadership and guidance of Apostle Dr. Deborah Dancy. Today, Monica is the director of sales for Deborah Dancy Ministries and is the Intercessory Prayer Team Leader at Jehovah Shalom International Kingdom Ministries. Recently, Monica has been designated to enter the inaugural cohort for the School of Apostles to expand her reach of God's Kingdom by helping others identify their callings and encouraging them to walk in the way God has called them.